John Smedley

by

John N. Merrill

Maps, photographs and pencil sketches by John N. Merrill

"I hike the footpaths and trails of the world for others to enjoy."

2010

My Derbyshire History Series
- Famous Derbyshire People

THE JOHN MERRILL FOUNDATION

THE JOHN MERRILL FOUNDATION

32, Holmesdale, Waltham Cross, Hertfordshire, England. EN8 8QY

Tel/Fax - 01992-762776
E-mail - marathonhiker@aol.com
www. johnmerrillwalkguides.com
www.pilgrimways.co.uk

A catalogue record for this book is available from the British Library.

Typset and designed by *The John Merrill Foundation*
Printed and handmade by ***John N. Merrill.***
Book layout and cover design by ***John N. Merrill***

ISBN 978 -1-903627-24-9
First published - March 2002. Reprinted - June 2009
Special limited edition.

Typeset in Humanst521 - bold, italic, and plain 11pt, 14pt and 18pt
Main titles in 18pt .**Humanst521 Bd BT** by John Merrill in Adobe Pagemaker on a iMac.

Please note - *The maps in this guide are purely illustrative. You are encouraged to use the appropriate 1:25,000 O.S. Explorer map as detailed on each walk.*

John Merrill confirms he has walked all the routes in this book and detailed what he found. Meticulous research has been undertaken to ensure that this publication is highly accurate at the time of going to press. The publishers, however, cannot be held responsible for alterations, errors, omissions, or for changes in details given. They would welcome information to help keep the book up to date.

Printed on paper from a 100% sustainable forest.
The John Merrill Foundation plants sufficient trees through the Woodland Trust to replenish the trees used in its publications.

ABOUT THE AUTHOR

Over the last 45 years John Merrill has walked over 200,000 miles - more than ten times around the world , wearing out 110 pairs of boots in the process. He has completed a remarkable and unequalled number of marathon walks - walking more than 28 miles per day on average - including being the first person to walk around Britain - 7,000 miles - in ten months. He has walked across Europe, Africa, India, Nepal, Asia, America, and along the great trails of America and Canada. He has completed many Pilgrim routes to Santiago de Compostela, Canterbury, Walsingham and Trondheim in Norway. Many more marathons and pilgrimages are planned.

He has written more than 340 guidebooks to his walks, most of which he prints and publishes himself. After his coast walk he realised the fame game prevented his from doing what he was destined to do, and that was to simply walk and write. He purposefully left the stage and concentrated on what he wanted to do. He does not consult anyone, promote or seek publicity; preferring to follow his own quiet spiritual path through life. This means he can write a book, on average one every month. He is not beholden to anyone, just a free spirit, with no staff, agents or editors. As a result he is not rich in money terms but in life and places walked to, a millionaire.

He is not a loner, quite the reverse, but to get the material and accomplish his walks - *"he who travels alone, travels fastest"*. And, by going alone you never forget. He is guided and has a very deep spiritual faith and has never come to any harm or put a foot wrong. The only way to be close to nature and mother earth and see its huge variety, is by walking; no other sport/exercise gives you that connectedness to the earth. He does no research beforehand, preferring to walk around the corner and come to a church, historic house, sacred site etc., and discover for himself their secrets. To be aware of what's next is to dampen the impact.

"A journey of a thousand miles, begins with a single step."
Lao Tzu (The Tao Te Ching).

I am on my third stage of my journey as an intuitive master, which continues daily - one life is not enough.

"Do not seek fame. Do not make plans.
Do not be absorbed by activities.
Do not think that you know.
Be aware of all that is and dwell in the infinite.
Wander where there is no path.
Be all that heaven gave you, but act as though
you have received nothing.
Be empty, that is all." Chuang Tzu

On July 17th. 2010 he was Ordained as an Interfaith Minister. see - **www.interfaithfoundation.org** for more details.

CONTENTS

INTRODUCTION

John Smedley, 1803 - 1874, was born in Wirksworth into the hosiery business. He continued his father's business in Lea Mills, becoming a very successful and inventive businessman. In mid-life, following an illness cured by hydropathy, he continued his mill work but devoted most of his time to his spiritual beliefs and to hydropathy. More than 100 years later Matlock is dominated by his "Smedley's Hydro" and Riber Castle; both of which he designed and saw to its construction. His mill still flourish's producing high quality knitwear.

His life story is fascinating and in his quiet way was one of Derbyshire's principal Victorian's. He became known as "The Prophet of the Peak" and as the "Father of Matlock Spa." Both are deserving titles, but he was more than that, a genius in his own right. This book briefly tells of his life and a seven mile walk, from his mill brings you to the key features of his life.

Happy exploring and walking!

A brief story of the life of John Smedley - 1803 - 1874

Born on 12th June 1803, the son of George Smedley of Wirksworth, who had a small hosiery business there. There appears to be no surviving papers relating to his early life. The early time of the family business was a struggle and his brother Isaac, a hosier wholesaler in London, went bankrupt and lost his house. But the quality of Smedley's work was such that other people helped to get him back into business. By 1818 the business premisses in Wirksworth were too small for the expanding business. As a result his father Leased larger premises at nearby, Lea Mills from the Nightingale family. In the mid 1820's the business, which had ebbed and flowed, was *"in a state of insolvency for the second time."* The business survived, just, but in 1827 the youngest son died and George Smedley lost interest in the business. It appears that John Smedley took over from his father. Despite little schooling, he had left school at fourteen, *"to assist his father in his business".* John Smedley would prove to have a natural flair for business and a clever engineer. His father died in 1840, by which time the business was booming and very well established.

Between 1823 and 1846 John Smedley devoted himself to the business and established it in the forefront of quality knitwear. He spent hours and days alone working out how to convert cotton machinery to woollen manufacture. This he achieved by carefully studying how the machines worked and how to adapt them to wool. By 1846 he had overcome all the obstacles and created a high quality market for the garments. He was also very kind to his employees, providing the women with capes for walking home in on wet days. In snowy winters he made arrangements for them to stay in comfort overnight in the mill. He also paid wages when employees were ill and provided them free with *"Fearn's Family Pills".* The mill's weekly wage bill rose from £12 to £200, during this period. He installed a manager to run the mill while he started the next phase of his life.

In 1846 he married, Caroline Anne Harward, the second daughter of the Vicar of Wirksworth. Their long honeymoon was spent in France and Switzerland. It was here that he caught a cold that developed into a fever. Back in England he tried conventional medicine to cure him, but it did not work. Eventually on advice he went to Dr. McCloed's hydropathy establishment, Ben Rhydding, in Harrogate and made a full recovery. The result changed his life as he began to promote the success and value of hydropathy. First he set up a small free hydropathy hospital at Lea Mills for his workers. He kept a woman there for 25 years costing between £500 - £750 per annum.

In 1853 he bought Mr. Davis's house on Matlock Bank - he was acting as medical adviser here - which he had used as a small hydropathic establishment, with eleven rooms and six patients. This would grow into Smedley's Hydro. With his wife they worked hard and long hours at the hydro and was run *"to make it neither a source of pecuniary emolument or of loss."*

He died on July 27th 1874 and his fortune was valid at over £100,000. His grave is near Holloway chapel and above his grave is an obelisk erected by his employees.

Having made a full recovery from the fever, he changed spiritually and hydropathy and religion became his principal activities. He often criticised the established church and wrote many pamphlets. Whilst never becoming ordained he became his "own" minister preaching his own form of Methodism, known as Wesleyan Reform. He designed and had built chapels at Matlock Bank, Bonsall, Birchwood (Alfreton), Holloway (built in 1852/3, enlarged in 1878 and now used as a Trinity Methodist church) and Higham; at a cost of between £5,000 and £10,000. He often went round villages with a marquee preaching his brand of religion, with a choir. He became known as the *"Prophet of the Peak."* He devised his own prayer book which was used in his chapels, but if the congregation disapproved of it, he removed it.

Combined John Smedley was unique and very much his own man and master of many talents - businessman, "inventor", amateur doctor, spiritual teacher, designer, architect and clerk of the works to all his building projects. This is one man you could not pigeon hole. Modesty seems to have been his motto for unlike other Famous Derbyshire People, he was never knighted or decorated. He was held in very high esteem locally, and his funeral procession from Riber Castle to Holloway, hundreds of people watched the cortege go by, which included eight mourning coaches. The service in Holloway Chapel was conducted by his great friend and workman, George Baker, head of the machine shop at Lea Mills; a post he held for 35 years. Around the cemetery it was estimated that *"There must have been some four thousand people present."* I fitting testimony to a great man.

John Smedley's obelisk in Holloway cemetery.

First morning at the Water Cure,
(Bathman brings the Wet sheet.)
"But I am sure I shall get my death of cold."

HYDROPATHY

"The Water Cure". "The treatment of disorders by external and internal application of water." There is no "curative" or "special" water in Matlock and as a result just ordinary hot and cold water was used. Smedley's experience of the very cold water at Ben Rhydding, determined him to use a "warmer" water in his treatments. The equipment used was designed by John Smedley and his book - *"Practical Hydropathy"*, has many illustrations of more than 200 types of bath. These include, a foot bath, hand bath, leg bath, shallow bath and douche bath. His wife Caroline wrote a *"Manual of Practical Hydropathy for Ladies and Children."*

Rock & Co London 0208

THE DOUCHE.

" Oh! Oh! Oh! Oh! "

Some of his patients wrote to him -

"A number of the patients in your hydropathic establishment feel desirous of expressing their sincere gratitude for the benefits they have personally received, and their great admiration of the knowledge and skill displayed in your application of the curative powers of water."

John Smedley claimed he could cure many ailments including venereal disease, diphtheria and lockjaw. He only dealt with external application of his treatments. In serious cases he used chilli paste and mustard. He was not a supporter of the use of leeches. John Smedley known as the *"Father of Matlock Spa"*, saw the growth of hydropathy in the Matlock area with nine establishments. Rockside Hydro was opened in 1862 by Charles Rowland.

ROCKSIDE

HYDROPATHIC AND BOARDING ESTABLISHMENT,

MATLOCK BANK, DERBYSHIRE.

This Institution, so well known for nearly thirty years as a Happy and Genial Home, both for Patients and Visitors, is situated on an eminence amidst the most beautiful scenery of Derbyshire, so well known as the Switzerland of England—its delightful and health-giving breezes in the Summer, with its sheltered and bracing air in the Winter, making it quite an all-the-year-round most delightful residence. A full descriptive circular post free on application to the Proprietor.

WM. ATKINS, *Resident Proprietor.*

THE FIRST HYDRO UPON MATLOCK BANK.

SMEDLEY'S HYDRO

The first hydro on Matlock Bank was opened by Ralph Davis of Darley dale in 1851. Two years later John Smedley bought the eleven roomed house, which was capable of treating six patients. The treatment proved to be very successful and within six years (1859), the building had been extensively enlarged to 76 bedrooms. John Smedley proved his designing skills, designing and supervising the extensions himself. The building continued to grow throughout the remainder of the 19th century to today's present edifice. He was an admirer of stained glass and used it extensively; there is a memorial window to him.

In 1863 there were more than 1,000 cases treated at the hydro, per year. Four years later, when the building was enlarged further to 94 bedrooms, the number had increased dramatically. At the time of death in 1874, the figure had risen to 3,000 cases per annum.

John Smedley insisted on a regimented life at the hydro, and amongst the his rules were -

"No books, newspapers, or tracts of irreligious character allowed, nor any newspapers on the Sabbath."

"Letter bag not sent for on Sabbath."

"Establishment strictly closed to visitors on the Sabbath"

"No alcohol or tobacco allowed."

Religious practice was observed with both morning and evening family worship. Fines were introduced to ensure compliance with establishment rules. These included -

1d. fine for coming to a meal after the blessing had been said.

10s 6d (52 1/2p) fine if a male guest entered the ladies sitting room.

In 1872 John Smedley handed over control of the hydro to Dr. William Bell Hunter, who continued his tradition for the next 22 years until his death in 1894.

Following John Smedley's death in 1874, the hydro became a company - "The Smedley's Hydropathic Co. Ltd." The hydro continued to expand and in 1881 the main staircase and entrance hall was built at a cost of £30,000. Five years later in 1886 the present front of the building was added. Soon afterwards pleasure gardens with walks, tennis courts and croquet lawns were constructed. The regimented life in hydro eased with a billiard room and dancing was allowed at Christmas together with a Christmas dinner and firework display. Later both alcohol and tobacco were allowed on the premises.

By the beginning of the 20th. century the hydro was at its zenith with bedroom accommodation for 300 and facilities equivalent to first class hotel. In 1897 a cable tramway was built up Bank Road, from Crown Square to Wellington Street. This closed in 1927. In the park opposite Crown Square can be seen the tramway shelter that once stood in Crown Square. Looking up Bank Road you can see the road bulge in the middle where the trams crossed. The fare was *"tuppence up the bank and penny down."*

In the early 1900's the hydro continued to expand and be full of people seeking the healthy cure. World War 1 saw the hydro used as a hospital. After the war it resumed its work, with many notable people staying, including Sir Thomas Beecham, Sir Harry Lauder and Bramwell

THE PRESENT
SMEDLEY HYDROPATHIC INSTITUTION

Booth, the son of William Booth, the founder of the Salvation Army. At the start of the second world war, it was aquisitioned by the War Department as a Military School of Intelligence. After the war it reopened briefly, but hydropathy was no longer popular. In 1956 the buildings were purchased by the Derbyshire County Council as there administrative headquarters; officially opened on 28th April 1956 by Alderman Charles White, CBE, JP.

A three storey high stained glass window beside the main staircase is in memory of John Smedley, dated 1882 and made by Shrigley and Hunt. The window cost £380 and the money was raised by public subscription. The inscription states he was born in 1804 and died in 1875, whereas infact he was born in 1803 and died 1874! The window depicts the healing power of water, which attracted so many to hydropathy.

The lower floor section records -

The left-hand window portrays Hygeia, the Goddess of Health, with latin inscription meaning - *"a healthy mind is a healthy body."*

The centre window portrays "truth", with a portrait of John Smedley - *" Great is the Truth and it will Prevail."*

The right-hand window portrays, Esculapius, the Greek God of Medicine - *"Hasten to meet disease as it comes."*

The middle floor section details the Pool of Bethesda, with Jesus and St. John healing a sick man.

The upper floor section has three female figures representing - Pure Air, Pure Water and Exercise. Across the window are the words - *"Welcome the coming, speed the parting guest."*

SMEDLEY'S
Hydropathic ∴ Establishment,
MATLOCK BRIDGE,
DERBYSHIRE.

ESTABLISHED 1853.

RAILWAY STATION, MATLOCK BRIDGE

(Between Matlock Bath and Darley Stations).

POSTAL & TELEGRAPH OFFICE, MATLOCK BANK.

For fuller Prospectus apply to Manager.

Printed by McCorquodale & Co., Ltd., Leeds.

Smedley's Hydropathic Establishment

IS pleasantly and healthily situated on the south-western aspect of a range of hills, overlooking the valley of the Derwent. It commands a view of great beauty bounded by the High Tor, Masson, and Riber hills, the latter capped by Riber Castle. The house is well sheltered from north and east by pine-clad hills, beyond which stretch moorland and forest for many miles. The aspect (south-west) and altitude (450 feet above the sea-level) secure a dry and bracing climate, but with sufficient shelter from the more rigorous winds. The district being mainly pastoral and remote from any great town, is well adapted for the purposes of a Sanatorium.

Within easy access lie the High Tor; the Vale of Matlock, with its wooded heights and gloomy caverns; the celebrated ducal palace of Chatsworth; the unique Haddon Hall; the quaint Hardwick Hall; Dove Dale, praised of Isaac Walton; Castleton, with its cavern and castle of the Peak; the towns of Bakewell and Buxton; the lovely Lathkil Dale; Miller and Monsal Dales; Lea Hurst, the birthplace of Florence Nightingale; and Wingfield Manor, a majestic ruin associated with the memory of Mary Queen of Scots.

As a Winter residence, the situation and size, the careful heating and ventilating (cared for constantly by the house attendant, under medical supervision), and the unfailing social liveliness of this Establishment, render it exceptionally suitable for invalids who might otherwise have had to winter abroad. Weeks may be passed indoors, in adverse weather, without much drawback to health, and on the numerous balconies and extensive promenades, covered and open, the most delicate can with safety take advantage of interlndes of fine weather, however brief.

Boating, fishing, and riding can be had, and there are the usual facilities for lawn tennis and other outdoor games.

NOTICE.—Rooms should, as far as possible, be engaged some days in advance of arrival, by intimation to the Matron, to whom also the date of departure should be communicated as early as convenient. Address Letters, Telegrams, &c., to MATLOCK BANK.

Terms.

The Baths are open free of charge to visitors and patients alike.

GENERAL TARIFF.

		£	s.	d.		£	s.	d.
Board, lodging, and bathing, according to situation of bedroom	per week	2	12	6	to	4	4	0
Ditto, when two persons occupy the same room	,, each	2	10	0	,,	3	19	0

Ditto, for children between six and twelve years of age, half-price.
Private sitting-rooms from £2 2s. 0d. per week.
Board for servants—female, 5s. per day; male, 6s. per day.

N.B.—Rooms when reserved from a certain date (or retained during a temporary absence) are charged half-price from the day they were engaged for occupation.

EXCEPTIONAL CHARGES.

Fire in private room for whole day, 1s.; evening only, 9d.
Serving meals (unless by medical orders) in private rooms—
Breakfast, per week, 2s. 6d.; all meals, 5s.

WINTER REDUCTIONS.

A reduction of 10 per cent. on the regular terms is allowed to all who reside in the Establishment for a period of one consecutive month or more between the 1st November and 1st March in each year. The reduction is made on each weekly bill, but comes into operation only at the end of November and is retrospective for that month. It can be claimed only after completion of the first month of residence in each case, and is then made for the whole month.

MEDICAL TARIFF.

Consultation fee (charged at first interview only, and covering subsequent advice as well as treatment) .. .. One guinea
Consultation fee for Out-Patients at each interview .. One guinea
Ditto ditto resident in the smaller establishments, 10s. 6d.

EXCEPTIONAL MEDICAL CHARGES.

		£	s.	d.
For special bathwoman	per week	1	1	0
Ditto bathman	,,	1	17	6
Rubber (female)	per hour	0	2	0
Ditto (male)	,,	0	3	0
For electric treatment	per application	0	1	0
Ditto	per hour	0	2	0

General Arrangements.

MEAL HOURS.

DAILY (Sundays excepted)—Breakfast, 8.30 a.m.; Dinner, 2.0 p.m.; Tea, 6.30 p.m.

For the more delicate invalids there are provided in the Saloon—Luncheon, 11.0 to 11.45 a.m.; Supper, 9.15 p.m.

SUNDAYS—Breakfast, 8.30 a.m.; Dinner, 1.0 p.m.; Tea, 5.30 p.m.; Supper, 9.15 p.m.

RELIGIOUS SERVICES.

Prayers in Drawing Room immediately after Breakfast, and at 9.0 p.m.

DRILL CLASS.

The Drill Instructor is in attendance from 9.30 to 11.0 a.m. every day except Sunday, to drill and exercise in calisthenics, single-stick, &c. Charge 1s. 6d. per week or portion of a week.

CHILDREN under six years of age cannot sometimes be admitted during the summer months, but accommodation may always be obtained for them in the houses of experienced and trustworthy persons in the neighbourhood.

NO FEES are allowed to be paid servants or bath attendants. The Directors are most anxious that this rule should be observed.

PRIVATE DINING ROOM.—Delicate cases, and such as are in any way unfit for the public table, have meals provided for them in a special apartment.

NIGHT WATCHMEN are in constant attendance throughout the night, and perambulate the buildings at stated intervals.

DOGS and other animal pets cannot under any circumstances be admitted.

THE GENERAL OFFICE is open daily (Sundays excepted) from 9.0 a.m. to 5.30 p.m.; on Saturdays till 2.0 p.m.

THE WEEKLY ACCOUNTS are rendered every Wednesday. Payment is requested in the office.

ARTICLES OF VALUE.—The Company will not hold themselves responsible for valuables unless deposited with Cashier for safe custody.

THE MANAGER AND MATRON will afford every attention and information to patients and visitors, and it is requested that all COMPLAINTS of negligence, inattention, and other irregularity, be made to them as soon after their occurrence as convenient, or addressed to the Chairman.

Medical Department.

Physicians.

WILLIAM B. HUNTER, M.D., &c.
JOS. G. G. CORKHILL, M.B., M.R.C.S. Eng., &c.

CONSULTATION ARRANGEMENTS.

NOTICE.—Intending patients should, on arrival, communicate with the Head Bath Attendant, who will arrange for a consultation. *New Arrivals* are seen by Dr. HUNTER at 10.30 a.m., and by Dr. CORKHILL at 5.0 p.m.

HOURS OF CONSULTATION.—*The regular weekly Consultations* are held between the hours of 3.0 and 5.0 p.m. with Dr. HUNTER; and between 5.0 and 6.30 p.m. with Dr. CORKHILL daily, Sundays excepted.

The Ladies' days for Dr. HUNTER are—Tuesdays, Thursdays, and Saturdays; the *Gentlemen's*—Mondays, Wednesdays, and Fridays. With Dr. CORKHILL the above order is reversed.

Questions of precedence are determined according to seniority on the consultation roll in the hands of the footman.

The Bathing Staff numbers in all from 35 to 40 skilled attendants, comprising a Head Bathman and Head Bathwoman, bathmen and bathwomen, special nurses (male and female), masseurs and masseuses, and electricians (male and female).

Attendance in the *Bathhouses* is as follows:—

Before Breakfast, from 6.30 a.m. till 8.15 a.m.
Forenoon, from 10.0 a.m. till 1.0 p.m.
Afternoon, from 3.0 p.m. till 5.0 p.m.
Evening, from 8.0 p.m. till 9.30 p.m.

Attendance in *Turkish and Russian Baths* is as follows:—

For Gentlemen, from 6.30 a.m. till 8.0 a.m.,
and from 9.30 a.m. till 2.0 p.m.
For Ladies, from 3.0 p.m. till 6.30 p.m., Saturdays excepted.

MASSAGE AND ELECTRICITY.—The Rubbers and Electricians are available by appointment, the hour being arranged by the Head Bath Attendant.

The Night-Watchmen are competent to give treatment in cases of need, and through them assistance may be had at any hour of the night.

OUT-PATIENTS.—The hour for Consultations with *Out-Patients* is 4.0 p.m.

For particulars of Medical Charges, see page 3.

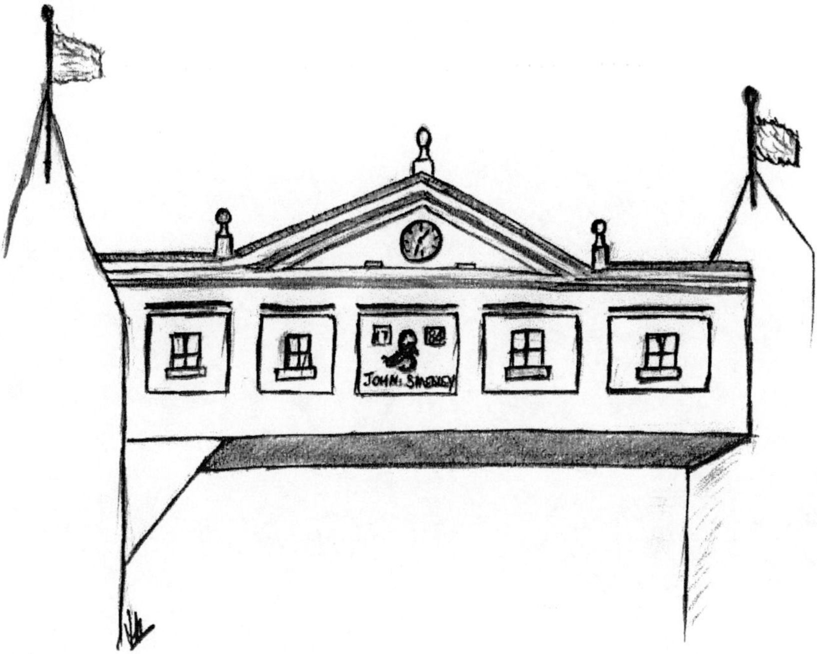

LEA MILLS

Located near a 14th century medieval water corn mill site. The original mill was built by Peter Nightingale in 1784, as a rival to Arkwright's mill at Cromford. Close by are the workers cottages. George Smedley leased it from Peter Nightingale in 1818 and later it was bought by John Smedley in the 1840's. It is interesting to note that the fourth John Smedley - John Bertram Marsden-Smedley - took control of the mill on his 21st. birthday. He remained Managing Director for over seventy years - almost a U.K. record - until an accident in 1959.

John Smedley had very good labour relations with his workers and proved a sympathetic and generous owner. Apart from the free hydropathy, he provided them with breakfast at 5d (2p) per week, consisting of Scottish porridge and golden syrup. His workers, about 350, were expected to observe his religious views, with morning prayers. In winter they were held inside the mill and in summer in a marquee.

John Smedley's house at Lea Mills.

RIBER CASTLE

John Smedley lived at Lea near the mill but later used Riber Hall, owned by his friend, George Allen, calling it his "summer retreat." He liked Riber very much and at first built a lodge here in 1863. Soon afterwards, having bought pieces of land from several people, he was able to start building the castle on the summit of the hill with its magnificent view of the Derwent Valley and to his hydro. The building was designed by John Smedley and built between 1862 - 8 and cost about £70,000. He was also on site to overview the construction, acting as the architect, engineer and clerk of works. The embattled castle was four angle towers and an embattled curtain wall with angle turrets. The castle is 145 feet long by 110 feet wide. Following his death in 1874 his wife, Caroline lived here for a total of thirty years until her death in 1892, when it was sold. In 1936 it was sold to Matlock U.D.C. for £1,150!

The castle is said to be haunted by two ghosts. The first is a military figure who marches through the walls. The second is a blue lady who wanders through the corridors and rooms.

Riber Lodge.

Smedley's coat of arms.

HOLLOWAY METHODIST CHURCH

Originally built by John Smedley in 1852 - you can see the date stone over the doorway with the initials, "C I S 1852." The C stands for his wife, Caroline. The I is that Latin capital for J - John. Above the stone is a circular recess believed to be for a clock, but it is unknown whether one was fitted. Above this is the bell tower which once had a bell, inscribed with the words - "Holloway Methodist." But it was too heavy and removed. Below the date stone, partially obliterated is the word - "Addition 1878". This was done four years after John Smedley's death, when the church was doubled in size.

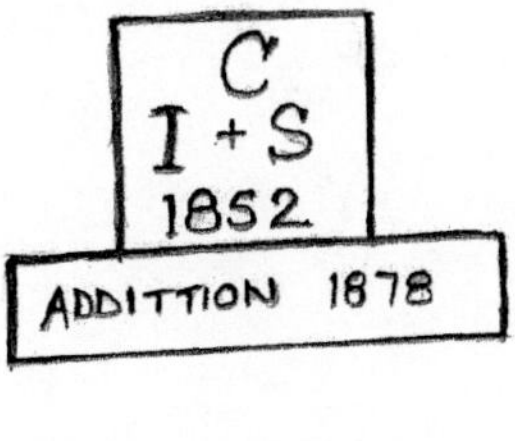

JOHN SMEDLEY WALK - 7 MILES

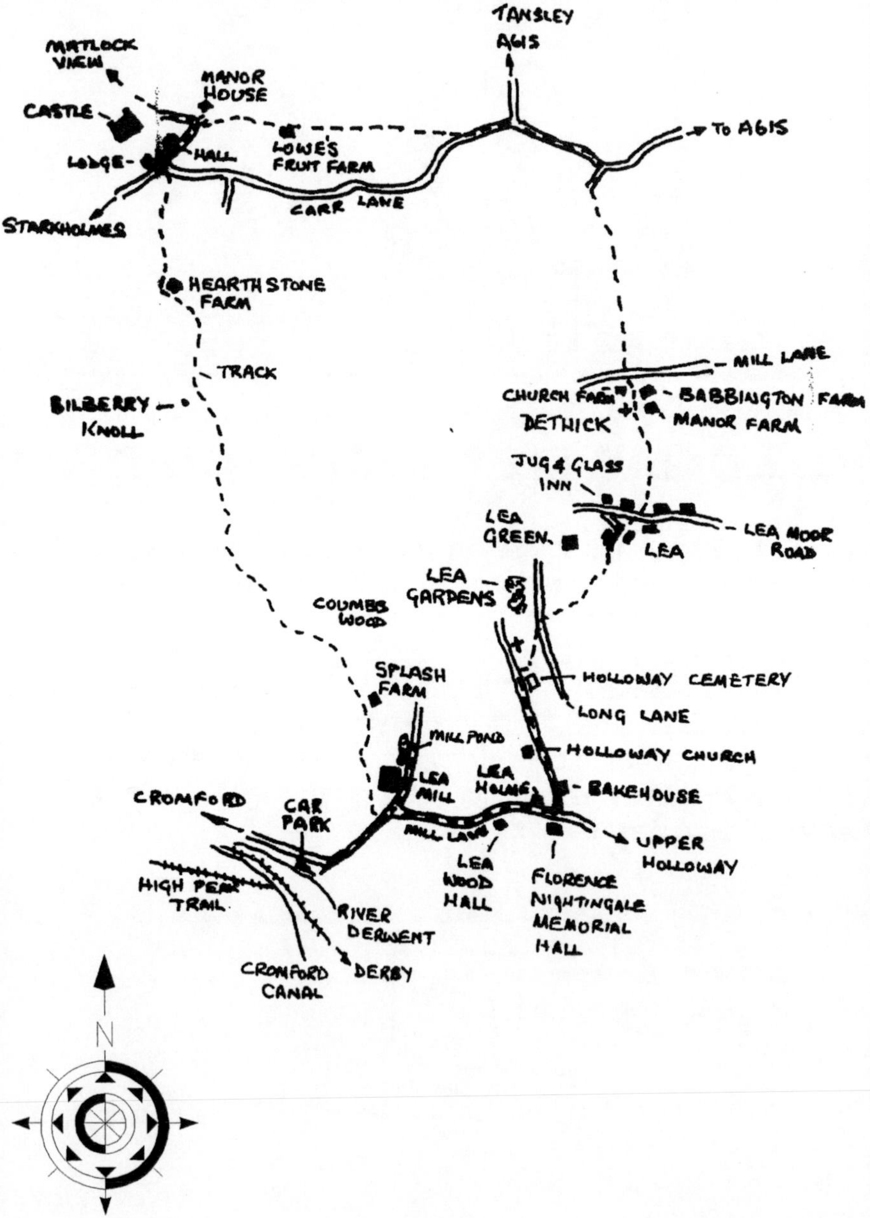

JOHN SMEDLEY WALK
- 7 MILES
- allow 3 to 4 hours.

Route - High Peak Junction Car Park - Lea Bridge - Holloway - Lea - Dethick - Riber - Hearthstone Farm - Bilberry Knoll - Hearthstone Lane - Coumbs Wood - Splash Farm - Lea Bridge - High Peak Junction Car Park.

O.S. MAP ***- 1:25,000 Outdoor Leisure Map No. 24 - The White Peak - East Sheet.***

VISITOR PARKING ***and start - High Peak Junction, off Lea Bridge Road. Grid Ref. SK315561.***

- The Jug & Glass Inn, Lea.

ABOUT THE WALK - From the car park you ascend gently to Lea Bridge and explore John Smedley's mill complex. From here you ascend more steeply to Holloway to see the chapel that he bulit in 1852. 300 yards later you reach his obelisk in the cemetery. A short ascend through beech trees brings you to Lea Rhododendron Gardens before walking into Lea. You continue to the fascinating hamlet of Dethick before crossing the fields to Riber to see the castle and lodge that he built. To return you follow Hearthstone Lane over the stunning vantage point of Bilberry Knoll before descending past Splash Farm to Lea Bridge. As you do so you have a good view over the Lea Mill complex. You retrace your steps back to the car park.

WALKING INSTRUCTIONS - Exit the far left-hand side of the car park onto a path to the bridge over the River Derwent. Don't cross, turn left along a tarmaced wooded path to the Lea Bridge road. Turn right along the road, passing Lea Wood House on your right. In 1/4 mile reach the start of John Smedley's mill and Mill Lane on your right. You ascend this but first continue ahead on the Lea road through the mill complex to explore the buildings and memorials to workers who died in both world wars. Beyond the buildings on the left is the mill pond. (On your return you approach the mill from the western side and retrace your steps back to the car park.) Return to Mill Lane and ascend passing Hollins Wood Close on your left and Lea Wood Hall on your right. Just after pass Lea Holme on your left and just after on your left is a historical plaque of the area, with the Florence Nightingale Memorial Hall on your right. You will come to four of these plaques on this walk. Turn left along Church Street, passing the former Bakehouse on your right. Then the Post Office on your left before John Smedley's - Holloway Methodist Church. Continue along the road and soon get views to your left of Lea Mill. Pass a toilet block on your right and a short distance later is the gate into the cemetery. Just to your left is the obelisk memorial to John Smedley and his wide Caroline.

Continue along the road a few more yards and pass Kirkdale house on your right. Just after turn right, as footpath signed, and ascend the cobbled path, and bear left on the ascending path walking through a splendid beech woodland. At the top gain Long Lane, with Lea Rhododendron Gardens on your left. Go straight across, as path signed, and walk beside the perimeter wall of Lea Green on your left. At the end reaching a track beside the path sign - Holloway, turn left past the houses to Holt Lane. Follow it round left and take the path on the right across the right-hand side of the playing fields. There is another historical plaque here and to your left is the Jug and Glass Inn. Gaining the road - Lea Moor Road - turn right then left at the path sign - Dethick - and descend steps to a bridge over a stream before ascending more and passing through rhododendrons to a stile. Turn left along the left-hand side of the field to a stile and onto Dethick church. Bear right past it along a path into Dethick hamlet with Manor Farm on your right. Turn left down the drive with Church Farm on your left to Dethick Lane.

Go straight across to a stile and path sign. Keep the wall on your left to come to four stiles. After this the path swings right, away from the wall to a stile and track. Turn right along the track to a lane and turn left. In 1/4 mile pass a lane to Tansley on your right and in a further 300 yards, now on Carr Lane, where the lane turns sharp left is a stile on your right. You are now heading due west for Riber. Basically keep a wall on your left to pass through five stiles before reaching the house of Lowes Fruit Farm on your left and the fruit bushes on your right. Here gain the farm drive and follow it for a short distance to a stile and path sign - Riber - on your left. Go through and keep the wall on your left to the next stile. Turn left then right to a stile onto the road at Riber. Your route is now left but first turn right - infront of you is Riber Manor dated 1633, but includes part of an earlier building. In a few yards turn left and ascend the road towards Riber Castle, taking the path at the top around the fence to see the view down onto Matlock and Smedley's Hydro. On your left is the impressive Riber Castle.

Retrace your steps back to the road and turn right passing Riber Hall on your right and then Riber Lodge. On the left is a well, pond and fenced Ordnance Survey enclosure, with the height stone - 797.28 feet. Turn left into Carr Lane, and immediately turn right through a stile and follow a defined path, heading southwards, to a wall on your right. Continue beside it coming to several stiles before gaining the drive via a stile by a path sign at Hearthstone farm. Turn left passing the farm on your left and soon walking on a walled track. Follow it as it swings right up a slight rise to the gritstone boulders of Bilberry Knoll on your right. Continue on the track - Hearthstone Lane - and soon have exceptional views on your left to Dethick, Lea and Crich. Descend the lane for nearly 1/2 mile to woodland on your right. Where the track bears right and descends in woodland, keep left on another track which almost immediately peters out. Here the path forks and keep left descending into a small disused quarry and pass a building on your right to a stile. Continue descending through woodland to a stile and bear left, following a defined path passing a marshy area on your right. Follow the path down to a wall on your left and onto a metal gate. Continue to another and as you approach Splash farm, take the stiled path on the right past it to another to gain the farm drive. Follow it to the next field boundary and through a stile on your right. Continue descending the left-hand side of the field, contouring round with Lea Mill on your left, to a stile and path sign on your left. Go through and bear right to the road at Lea Bridge. Turn right and descend the road retracing your steps back to Lea Wood House. Just after turn left onto the tarmaced path to return to the car park.

LEA GREEN - Originally a 17th century farmhouse enlarged and extended in 1908 by John B. Marsden-Smedley. He also created Lea Rhododendron Gardens.

JOHN SMEDLEY OBELISK - In the cemetery, on land provided by the Nightingale and Shore family of Lea Hurst, 300 yards from Holloway Church; on entering on the left is the obelisk and memorial provided by his employees. The side panels read -

> *"In memory of John Smedley of Riber Castle and Lea Mills who fell asleep in Jesus, July 27th. 1874 Aged 71 years." "I am the resurrection and the life he that liveth and beliveth in me shall never die."*
>
> *"In memory of Caroline Ann his devoted wife who died February 26th 1892 Aged 69 years. " "She hath done what she could."*
>
> *"Erected by the employees in remembrance of his unceasing kindness, liberality and care for their welfare."*

The mortuary was erected at the expense of Mr. Wass of the Green Inn, with the balance raised by public subscription.

Reference Sources -

The Spas of England by P.J.N. Havins

Booklet - John Smedley - 1803-1874 - Centenary Exhibition

John Smedley by S.W.Partridge

The Smedley's of Matlock Bank by Henry Steer. Elliot Stock. 1897

John Smedley of Matlock and his Hydro by L. du Garde Peach

Allison Uttley's Country Walks by Freda Bayles

Derbyshire Life & Countryside - Vol. 45 No. 4 - April 1980

Recollections of the late John Smedley by J. Buckley. John Heywood 1888.

Derbyshire. Pevsner

Derbyshire County Council sheets on “County Hall” and “Stained Glass Window.”

The Water Cure - a 19th, century cartoon booklet.

FAMOUS DERBYSHIRE PEOPLE SERIES
by John Merrill

- each guide book is 40 to 72 pages long, with the story of the person with maps, sketches and illustrations. Also in included is a detailed walk of about 4 to 5 miles around the area the subject lived, seeing at first hand where history was made.

SIR RICHARD ARKWRIGHT OF CROMFORD - the cotton spinning genius who revolutionised industry.

SIR JOSEPH PAXTON - Gardener to the Sixth Duke of Devonshire, who designed the village of Edensor and the Crystal Palace for the 1851 Great Exhibition.

FLORENCE NIGHTINGALE - The Lady with the lamp - the Heroine of the Crimea War and the founder of modern nursing.

JOHN SMEDLEY - The creator of Smedley's Hydro, Riber castle and Lea Mills.

BONNIE PRINCE CHARLIE - the story of march through Derbyshire to Derby, on his attempt to regain the English crown, in 1745. Includes walking instructions to the 21 mile "Bonnie Prince Charlie Walk", from Ashbourne to Derby.

THE STORY OF THE EARLS & DUKES OF DEVONSHIRE - The Cavendish family, from Bess of Hardwick through the Earls of Devonshire and the Dukes of Devonshire to the present time. Includes a walk around Chatsworth and Hardwick.

In preparation -

BESS OF HARDWICK - The Costly Countess - Builder of Hardwick Hall and "goaler" of Mary Queen of Scots.

MARY QUEEN OF SCOTS - "The Captive Queen" - The story of her fiften year imprisonment in Derbyshire, including the Babington Plot, before being beheaded.

John Merrill's - "My Derbyshire" Historical Series.

A TO Z GUIDE TO THE PEAK DISTRICT by John N. Merrill
WINSTER - A SOUVENIR GUIDE .by John N. Merrill
DERBYSHIRE INNS - an A TO Z GUIDE . by John N. Merrill
HALLS & CASTLES OF THE PEAK DISTRICT. by John N. Merrill.
DERBYSHIRE FACTS AND RECORDS by John N. Merrill
THE STORY OF THE EYAM PLAGUE by Clarence Daniel
THE EYAM DISCOVERY TRAIL by Clarence Daniel
PEAK DISTRICT SKETCHBOOKby John N. Merrill
LOST DERBYSHIRE VILLAGE WALKS - VOL 1 & 2 by John N. Merrill
TOURING THE PEAK DISTRICY & DERBYSHIRE BY CAR by John N. Merrill
LOST INDUSTRIES OF DERBYSHIRE by John N. Merrill
DERBYSHIRE LOST VILLAGE WALK - Vols. 1 & 2 by John N. Merrill
DESERTED MEDIEVAL VILLAGES OF DERBYSHIRE by John N. Merrill
MANORS & FAMILIES OF DERBYSHIRE - Vol 1 - A to L - Photographed & edited by
MANORS & FAMILES OF DERBYSHIRE -Vol 2 - M to Z - John N. Merrill
DERBYSHIRE PILGRIMAGES by John N. Merrill

FAMOUS DERBYSHIRE PEOPLE - each includes a 4 mile historical walk.

SIR RICHARD ARKWRIGHT OF CROMFORD by John N. Merrill.
SIR JOSEPH PAXTON by John N. Merrill
FLORENCE NIGHTINGALE by John N. Merrill
JOHN SMEDLEY by John N. Merrill
MARY QUEEN OF SCOTS - "The Captive Queen." by John N. Merrill
BESS OF HARDWICK - "The Costly Countess" by John N. Merrill
THE STORY OF THE EARLS AND DUKES OF DEVONSHIRE by John N. Merrill
BONNIE PRINCE CHARLIE & 20 mile walk by John N. Merrill

GHOSTS & LEGENDS -

DERBYSHIRE FOLKLORE.by John N. Merrill.
DERBYSHIRE PUNISHMENT by John N. Merrill.
CUSTOMS OF THE PEAK DISTRICT & DERBYS by John N. Merrill
LEGENDS OF DERBYSHIRE. by John N. Merrill.
GRANDFATHER THOMAS JACKSON'S VICTORIAN CURES & RECIPES

PEAK DISTRICT VISITOR'S GUIDES by John N. Merrill

ASHOURNE BAKEWELL MATLOCK THE HOPE VALLEY

DERBYSHIRE HISTORY THROUGH THE AGES -

Vol 1 - DERBYSHIRE IN PREHISTORIC TIMES & 13 mile walk by John N. Merrill
Vol 3 - DERBYSHIRE IN NORMAN TIMES by John N. Merrill
Vol 4 - DERBYSHIRE IN MONASTIC TIMES by John N. Merrill

OTHER JOHN MERRILL WALK BOOKS

CIRCULAR WALK GUIDES -
SHORT CIRCULAR WALKS IN THE PEAK DISTRICT - VOL. 1,2, 3 AND 9
CIRCULAR WALKS IN WESTERN PEAKLAND
SHORT CIRCULAR WALKS IN THE STAFFORDSHIRE MOORLANDS
SHORT CIRCULAR WALKS - TOWNS & VILLAGES OF THE PEAK DISTRICT
SHORT CIRCULAR WALKS AROUND MATLOCK
SHORT CIRCULAR WALKS IN "PEAK PRACTICE COUNTRY."
SHORT CIRCULAR WALKS IN THE DUKERIES
SHORT CIRCULAR WALKS IN SOUTH YORKSHIRE
SHORT CIRCULAR WALKS IN SOUTH DERBYSHIRE
SHORT CIRCULAR WALKS AROUND BUXTON
SHORT CIRCULAR WALKS AROUND WIRKSWORTH
SHORT CIRCULAR WALKS IN THE HOPE VALLEY
40 SHORT CIRCULAR WALKS IN THE PEAK DISTRICT
CIRCULAR WALKS ON KINDER & BLEAKLOW
SHORT CIRCULAR WALKS IN SOUTH NOTTINGHAMSHIRE
SHORT CIRCULAR WALKS IN CHESHIRE
SHORT CIRCULAR WALKS IN WEST YORKSHIRE
WHITE PEAK DISTRICT AIRCRAFT WRECKS
CIRCULAR WALKS IN THE DERBYSHIRE DALES
SHORT CIRCULAR WALKS FROM BAKEWELL
SHORT CIRCULAR WALKS IN LATHKILL DALE
CIRCULAR WALKS IN THE WHITE PEAK
SHORT CIRCULAR WALKS IN EAST DEVON
SHORT CIRCULAR WALKS AROUND HARROGATE
SHORT CIRCULAR WALKS IN CHARNWOOD FOREST
SHORT CIRCULAR WALKS AROUND CHESTERFIELD
SHORT CIRCULAR WALKS IN THE YORKS DALES - VOL 1 - SOUTHERN AREA.
SHORT CIRCULAR WALKS IN THE AMBER VALLEY (DERBYSHIRE)
SHORT CIRCULAR WALKS IN THE LAKE DISTRICT
SHORT CIRCULAR WALKS IN THE NORTH YORKSHIRE MOORS
SHORT CIRCULAR WALKS IN EAST STAFFORDSHIRE
LONG CIRCULAR WALKS IN THE PEAK DISTRICT - VOL.1, 2 , 3, 4 AND 5.
DARK PEAK AIRCRAFT WRECK WALKS
LONG CIRCULAR WALKS IN THE STAFFORDSHIRE MOORLANDS
LONG CIRCULAR WALKS IN CHESHIRE
WALKING THE TISSINGTON TRAIL
WALKING THE HIGH PEAK TRAIL
WALKING THE MONSAL TRAIL & SETT VALLEY TRAILS
PEAK DISTRICT WALKING - TEN "TEN MILER'S" - VOL ONE AND TWO
CLIMB THE PEAKS OF THE PEAK DISTRICT
PEAK DISTRICT WALK A MONTH VOLS ONE,TWO, THREE, FOUR, FIVE & SIX
TRAIN TO WALK VOL. ONE - THE HOPE VALLEY LINE
DERBYSHIRE LOST VILLAGE WALKS -VOL ONE AND TWO.
CIRCULAR WALKS IN DOVEDALE AND THE MANIFOLD VALLEY
CIRCULAR WALKS AROUND GLOSSOP
WALKING THE LONGDENDALE TRAIL
WALKING THE UPPER DON TRAIL
SHORT CIRCULAR WALKS IN CANNOCK CHASE
CIRCULAR WALKS IN THE DERWENT VALLEY
WALKING THE TRAILS OF NORTH-EAST DERBYSHIRE
WALKING THE PENNINE BRIDLEWAY & CIRCULAR WALKS
SHORT CIRCULAR WALKS ON THE NEW RIVER & SOUTH-EAST HERTFORDSHIRE
SHORT CIRCULAR WALKS IN EPPING FOREST
WALKING THE STREETS OF LONDON
LONG CIRCULAR WALKS IN EASTERN HERTFORDSHIRE
LONG CIRCULAR WALKS IN WESTERN HERTFORDSHIRE
WALKS IN THE LONDON BOROUGH OF ENFIELD
WALKS IN THE LONDON BOROUGH OF BARNET
WALKS IN THE LONDON BOROUGH OF HARINGEY
WALK IN THE LONDON BOROUGH OF WALTHAM FOREST
SHORT CIRCULAR WALKS AROUND HERTFORD
THE BIG WALKS OF LONDON
SHORT CIRCULAR WALKS AROUND BISHOP'S STORTFORD
SHORT CIRCULAR WALKS AROUND EPPING DISTRICT
CIRCULAR WALKS IN THE BOROUGH OF BROXBOURNE

CANAL WALKS -
VOL 1 - DERBYSHIRE & NOTTINGHAMSHIRE
VOL 2 - CHESHIRE & STAFFORDSHIRE
VOL 3 - STAFFORDSHIRE
VOL 4 - THE CHESHIRE RING
VOL 5 - THE GRANTHAM CANAL
VOL 6 - SOUTH YORKSHIRE
VOL 7 - THE TRENT & MERSEY CANAL
VOL 8 - WALKING THE DERBY CANAL RING
VOL 9 - WALKING THE LLANGOLLEN CANAL
VOL 10 - CIRCULAR WALKS ON THE CHESTERFIELD CANAL
VOL 11 - CIRCULAR WALKS ON THE CROMFORD CANAL
VOL.13 - SHORT CIRCULAR WALKS ON THE RIVER LEE NAVIGATION -VOL. 1 - NORTH
VOL. 14 - SHORT CIRCULAR WALKS ON THE RIVER STORT NAVIGATION
VOL.15 - SHORT CIRCULAR WALKS ON THE RIVER LEE NAVIGATION - VOL. 2 - SOUTH
VOL. 16 - WALKING THE CANALS OF LONDON
VOL 17 - WALKING THE RIVER LEE NAVIGATION
VOL. 20 - SHORT CIRCULAR WALKS IN THE COLNE VALLEY

JOHN MERRILL DAY CHALLENGE WALKS -
WHITE PEAK CHALLENGE WALK
THE HAPPY HIKER - WHITE PEAK - CHALLENGE WALK NO.2
DARK PEAK CHALLENGE WALK
PEAK DISTRICT END TO END WALKS
STAFFORDSHIRE MOORLANDS CHALLENGE WALK

THE LITTLE JOHN CHALLENGE WALK
YORKSHIRE DALES CHALLENGE WALK
NORTH YORKSHIRE MOORS CHALLENGE WALK
LAKELAND CHALLENGE WALK
THE RUTLAND WATER CHALLENGE WALK
MALVERN HILLS CHALLENGE WALK
THE SALTER'S WAY
THE SNOWDON CHALLENGE
CHARNWOOD FOREST CHALLENGE WALK
THREE COUNTIES CHALLENGE WALK (PEAK DISTRICT).
CAL-DER-WENT WALK BY GEOFFREY CARR,
THE QUANTOCK WAY
BELVOIR WITCHES CHALLENGE WALK
THE CARNEDDAU CHALLENGE WALK
THE SWEET PEA CHALLENGE WALK
THE LINCOLNSHIRE WOLDS - BLACK DEATH - CHALLENGE WALK
JENNIFER'S CHALLENGE WALK
THE EPPING FOREST CHALLENGE WALK
THE THREE BOROUGH CHALLENGE WALK - NORTH LONDON

INSTRUCTION & RECORD -
HIKE TO BE FIT.....STROLLING WITH JOHN
THE JOHN MERRILL WALK RECORD BOOK
HIKE THE WORLD - JOHN MERRILL'S GUIDE TO WALKING & BACKPACKING.

MULTIPLE DAY WALKS -
THE RIVERS'S WAY
PEAK DISTRICT: HIGH LEVEL ROUTE
PEAK DISTRICT MARATHONS
THE LIMEY WAY
THE PEAKLAND WAY
COMPO'S WAY BY ALAN HILEY
THE BRIGHTON WAY BY NORMAN WILLIS

THE PILGRIM WALKS SERIES -
THE WALSINGHAM WAY - ELY TO WALSINGHAM - 72 MILES
THE WALSINGHAM WAY - KINGS LYNN TO WALSINGHAM - 35 MILES
TURN LEFT AT GRANJA DE LA MORERUELA - 700 MILES
NORTH TO SANTIAGO DE COMPOSTELA, VIA FATIMA - 650 MILES
ST. OLAV'S WAY - OSLO TO TRONDHEIM - 400 MILES
ST. WINEFRIDE'S WAY - ST. ASAPH TO HOLYWELL
ST. ALBANS WAY - WALTHAM ABBEY TO ST. ALBANS - 26 MILES
ST. KENELM TRAIL BY JOHN PRICE - CLENT HILLS TO WINCHCOMBE - 60 MILES
DERBYSHIRE PILGRIMAGES
LONDON TO CANTERBURY- 75 MILES
LONDON TO ST. ALBANS - 36 MILES
LONDON TO WALSINGHAM - 194 MILES
FOLKESTONE, HYTHE TO CANTERBURY - 25 MILES
THE JOHN SCHORNE PEREGRINATIONS - 27 MILES BY M. MOONEY
ST CEDD'S PILGRIMAGE WALK - 24 MILES
ST BIRINIUS PILGRIMAGE WALK - 26 MILES

COAST WALKS & NATIONAL TRAILS -
ISLE OF WIGHT COAST PATH
PEMBROKESHIRE COAST PATH
THE CLEVELAND WAY
WALKING ANGELSEY'S COASTLINE.
WALKING THE COASTLINE OF THE CHANNEL ISLANDS
THE ISLE OF MAN COASTAL PATH - *"THE WAY OF THE GULL."*
A WALK AROUND HAYLING ISLAND
A WALK AROUND THE ISLE OF SHEPPEY
A WALK AROUND THE ISLE OF JERSEY

DERBYSHIRE & PEAK DISTRICT HISTORICAL GUIDES -
A TO Z GUIDE OF THE PEAK DISTRICT
DERBYSHIRE INNS - AN A TO Z GUIDE
HALLS AND CASTLES OF THE PEAK DISTRICT & DERBYSHIRE
TOURING THE PEAK DISTRICT & DERBYSHIRE BY CAR
DERBYSHIRE FOLKLORE
PUNISHMENT IN DERBYSHIRE
CUSTOMS OF THE PEAK DISTRICT & DERBYSHIRE
WINSTER - A SOUVENIR GUIDE
ARKWRIGHT OF CROMFORD
LEGENDS OF DERBYSHIRE
DERBYSHIRE FACTS & RECORDS
TALES FROM THE MINES BY GEOFFREY CARR
PEAK DISTRICT PLACE NAMES BY MARTIN SPRAY
DERBYSHIRE THROUGH THE AGES - VOL 1 -DERBYSHIRE IN PREHISTORIC TIMES
SIR JOSEPH PAXTON
FLORENCE NIGHTINGALE
JOHN SMEDLEY
BONNIE PRINCE CHARLIE & 20 MILE WALK.
THE STORY OF THE EARLS AND DUKES OF DEVONSHIRE

JOHN MERRILL'S MAJOR WALKS -
TURN RIGHT AT LAND'S END
WITH MUSTARD ON MY BACK
TURN RIGHT AT DEATH VALLEY
EMERALD COAST WALK
I CHOSE TO WALK - WHY I WALK ETC.
A WALK IN OHIO - 1,310 MILES AROUND THE BUCKEYE TRAIL.

SKETCH BOOKS -
SKETCHES OF THE PEAK DISTRICT

COLOUR BOOK:-
THE PEAK DISTRICT.......SOMETHING TO REMEMBER HER BY.

OVERSEAS GUIDES -
HIKING IN NEW MEXICO - VOL I - THE SANDIA AND MANZANO MOUNTAINS.
VOL 2 - HIKING "BILLY THE KID" COUNTRY. VOL 4 - N.W. AREA - " HIKING INDIAN COUNTRY."
"WALKING IN DRACULA COUNTRY" - ROMANIA.
WALKING THE TRAILS OF THE HONG KONG ISLANDS.

VISITOR GUIDES - MATLOCK . BAKEWELL. ASHBOURNE.

Notes ~